3 4028 08045 6107
HARRIS COUNTY PUBLIC LIBRARY

J 599.83 Cla
Clark, Willow
Bush babies

$8.25
ocn746489151
1st ed.   07/24/2012

Bush Babies

Willow Clark

D0945615

PowerKiDS press.

New York

Published in 2012 by The Rosen Publishing Group, Inc.
29 East 21st Street, New York, NY 10010

Copyright © 2012 by The Rosen Publishing Group, Inc.

All rights reserved. No part of this book may be reproduced in any form without permission in writing from the publisher, except by a reviewer.

First Edition

Editor: Joanne Randolph
Book Design: Greg Tucker
Layout Design: Julio Gil

Photo Credits: Cover Volkmar Wentzel/National Geographic/Getty Images; p. 4 © www. iStockphoto.com/Eliza Snow; p. 5 Anthony Bannister/Gallo Images/Getty Images; p. 6 © McPhoto/ age fotostock; pp. 7, 14–15 © Photoshot/age fotostock; p. 8 (left) Steve Turner/Oxford Scientific/ Getty Images; pp. 8 (right), 18, 19, 22 Shutterstock.com; p. 9 Federico Veronesi/Gallo Images/ Getty Images; p. 10 Rob Nunnington/Oxford Scientific/Getty Images; p. 11 © M. Bussmann/age fotostock; pp. 12–13 © Gerard Lacz/age fotostock; p. 16 © www.iStockphoto.com/Nico Smit; p. 17 Ariadne Van Zandbergen/Oxford Scientific/Getty Images; pp. 20–21 Gallo Images-Heinrich van den Berg/The Image Bank/Getty Images.

Library of Congress Cataloging-in-Publication Data

Clark, Willow.
 Bush babies / by Willow Clark. — 1st ed.
    p. cm. — (Up a tree)
 Includes index.
 ISBN 978-1-4488-6188-0 (library binding) — ISBN 978-1-4488-6335-8 (pbk.) —
 ISBN 978-1-4488-6336-5 (6-pack)
 1. Galagos—Juvenile literature. I. Title. II. Series.
 QL737.P937C55 2012
 599.8'3—dc23

                                                2011030050

Manufactured in the United States of America

CPSIA Compliance Information: Batch #WW12PK: For Further Information contact Rosen Publishing, New York, New York at 1-800-237-9932

Contents

Meet the Bush Baby

The bush baby, or galago, makes cries that can be heard ringing through the trees in many forests across Africa. It is one of the world's smallest **primates**. Primates are **mammals** that have well-developed brains. They also have hands and feet that can grip. Apes, monkeys, and people are all primates.

Bush babies come out mainly at night, so it is not common to see one out during the day, as this one is. This bush baby lives in Tanzania, in Africa.

Bush babies are **arboreal** animals. That means they spend most of their time in trees. They almost never

There are many kinds of bush babies in Africa. These two bush babies are called lesser galagos. This is one of the smallest kinds of galago.

come down to the ground. They do almost all of their eating, sleeping, and traveling in trees. This book will teach you more about the bush baby's tree-centered life.

How to Pick a Tree

Bush babies live in Africa in forests and bushlands south of the Sahara, as well as on the island of Zanzibar. Bush babies usually live in small groups, made up of a mother and her offspring. Groups come together to sleep but spend their waking hours alone.

When bush babies are together, they may bond with each other by grooming, or cleaning, each other's fur.

Bush babies look for trees that do not have a lot of grass growing on the ground around them. This keeps the bush baby safer if there is

This lesser galago is peeking out of its tree hollow. Tree hollows give a safe resting spot to a bush baby as it rests during the day.

a wildfire during a dry season. Bush babies like to live in the hollows of trees. They can stay hidden there. They may also build nests in the forks of tree branches, though. For an arboreal animal like the bush baby, picking a good tree is very important!

Bush Baby Bodies

Bush babies have brownish woolly fur and long tails. They are between the size of a squirrel and a small cat. Lesser galagos have large eyes and large, hairless, movable ears. These features help these **nocturnal** animals see and hear in the dark.

Bush babies make several different sounds to communicate with each other. They make noises

Left: The brown galago is one kind of greater bush baby. Greater galagos are also called thick-tailed bush babies because their tails are wider than other bush babies'. *Right*: The Mohol bush baby is one kind of lesser galago.

Here you can see this Senegal bush baby's large eyes and big ears. The shape of its ears helps it hear even very quiet sounds.

to find each other before going to sleep, to find **mates**, and to tell others about nearby **predators**.

Scientists have argued about how to sort bush babies, but generally agree that there are 14 **species**. These different species are similar to each other and are sometimes difficult for scientists to tell apart!

The Night Life

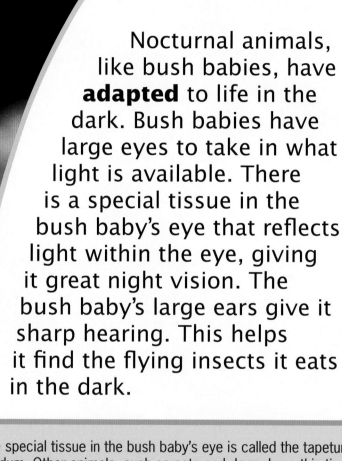

Nocturnal animals, like bush babies, have **adapted** to life in the dark. Bush babies have large eyes to take in what light is available. There is a special tissue in the bush baby's eye that reflects light within the eye, giving it great night vision. The bush baby's large ears give it sharp hearing. This helps it find the flying insects it eats in the dark.

The special tissue in the bush baby's eye is called the tapetum lucidum. Other animals, such as cats and dogs, have this tissue, too. This is what makes these animals' eyes shine in the dark.

Bush babies wake up about a half hour before nightfall. First they stretch and groom, or clean, themselves. Then

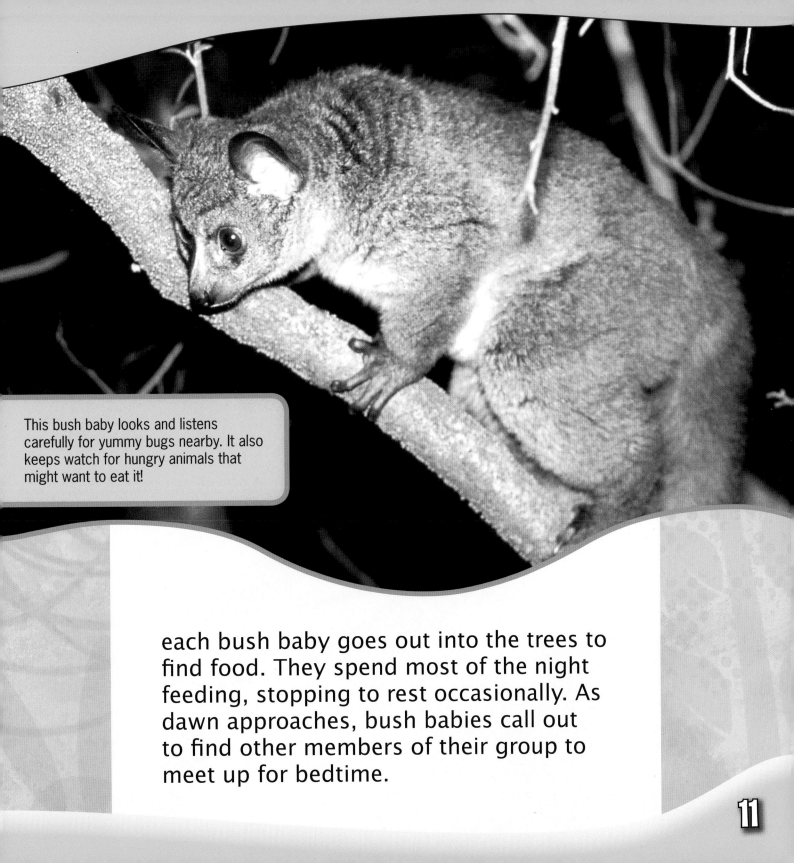

This bush baby looks and listens carefully for yummy bugs nearby. It also keeps watch for hungry animals that might want to eat it!

each bush baby goes out into the trees to find food. They spend most of the night feeding, stopping to rest occasionally. As dawn approaches, bush babies call out to find other members of their group to meet up for bedtime.

It's a Fact!

1

Galagos likely earned the nickname "bush baby" because their calls can sound like a baby's cries.

4

Bush babies fold their ears against their heads when they are sleeping.

7

Bush babies get the water they need from the foods they eat.

2

A bush baby's ears can move independently from each other. This lets bush babies hear sounds coming from different directions more clearly.

3

When two bush babies meet, they will touch noses to smell each other.

5

The bush baby's long tail helps it keep its balance while moving through the trees.

6

Adult male bush babies live alone. Bush baby groups are usually made up of two adult females and their offspring.

8

Chimpanzees sometimes use sharp sticks as tools to hunt bush babies.

9

Male bush babies do not play a role in raising young.

10

Female bush babies sometimes give birth to triplets. This is rare, though.

On the Move

A bush baby moves through trees by jumping, hopping, and walking. It jumps from one branch and grabs on to the next branch with all four feet. It also hops or walks along a branch on all four feet. The ends of its toes have a thick, flat layer of skin. This skin keeps the bush baby from slipping.

Bush babies move to other trees by jumping to them. They do this when they are looking for food or to get away from danger.

Bush babies also mark the trees with their scents as they move through them. This is called scent marking. To do this, they put urine on their feet, which marks the branches as they move. This allows them to use their noses to retrace their routes through the trees. Among male bush babies, scent marking also lets males know that another male is using certain trees.

Time to Eat!

Bush babies are **omnivores**. They eat mostly insects, as well as leaves, eggs, and fruit. They also eat the gum, or sticky sap, from acacia trees. They eat this gum mainly during **droughts**, when their other favorite foods are not as plentiful.

Bush babies locate **prey** by listening for them with their big ears, then looking in the direction of that sound with their sharp night vision. Then

The bush baby's favorite food is grasshoppers. They are most plentiful during the wet season.

This greater bush baby is munching on some leaves in Kenya.

they grab the prey with their front feet while gripping a branch with their back feet. Bush babies eat a tree's gum by scraping the tree with a special tooth on their lower jaw and licking with their tongues.

Bush Baby Predators

A small animal like the bush baby has many different kinds of predators. Owls, snakes, monkeys, chimpanzees, and catlike mammals, called genets, all prey on bush babies.

Genets live in many different African habitats and eat many different kinds of food, including small animals, such as the bush baby. Genets are related to mongooses.

The bush baby's best **defenses** are hiding, staying alert, and getting away from its predators. Bush babies' brown fur helps them stay camouflaged, or hidden in the trees. If a predator is nearby, they call out to let other bush babies know.

Chimpanzees eat mainly fruit, but they also eat insects, eggs, and meat. They often work together to hunt primates, such as the galago.

If a predator finds a bush baby in the trees, the bush baby can quickly jump away from it. A bush baby is in much greater danger from predators on the ground. This is the main reason they almost never leave the safety of the trees!

Mating and Babies

Male bush babies seek out a female or a group of females with which to mate. Females give birth about four months after mating.

> A mother may carry her young in her mouth or the baby may hang on to its mother's belly or back.

Females generally have only one baby at a time, although they sometimes have twins. The newborns weigh about .5 ounce (14 g). During its first few days, the mother keeps her baby close to her. Then she starts to leave it in her nest while she finds food. The mother nurses her young for about three months. After about two months, a young bush baby learns to feed itself. When they are about a year old, males leave their mothers, while females stay with their mothers' group.

Trouble Ahead?

Bush babies are sometimes sold as pets, but it is better to leave them in their natural homes.

The bush baby is not considered to be **endangered** because it is found over a wide range and is fairly common. However, its range is broken up into small, unconnected populations. This means that there can be places where the number of bush babies is falling, although the overall number of bush babies is somewhat large.

The biggest threat to bush babies is habitat loss. Forests are being cut down to make way for homes, roads, and businesses. This leaves bush babies with fewer places to live. In some countries, such as Kenya, bush babies or their habitat are **protected** by law.

Glossary

adapted (uh-DAPT-ed) Changed to fit conditions.

arboreal (ahr-BOR-ee-ul) Having to do with trees.

defenses (dih-FENTS-ez) Things a living thing does that help keep it safe.

droughts (DROWTS) Periods of dryness.

endangered (in-DAYN-jerd) In danger of no longer existing.

mammals (MA-mulz) Warm-blooded animals that have backbones and hair, breathe air, and feed milk to their young.

mates (MAYTS) Male and female animals that come together to make babies.

nocturnal (nok-TUR-nul) Active during the night.

omnivores (OM-nih-vawrz) Animals that eat both plants and animals.

predators (PREH-duh-terz) Animals that kill other animals for food.

prey (PRAY) An animal that is hunted by another animal for food.

primates (PRY-mayts) The group of animals that are more advanced than others and includes monkeys, gorillas, and humans.

protected (pruh-TEKT-ed) Kept safe.

species (SPEE-sheez) One kind of living thing. All people are one species.

Harris County Public Library
Houston, Texas

Index

Web Sites

Due to the changing nature of Internet links, PowerKids Press has developed an online list of Web sites related to the subject of this book. This site is updated regularly. Please use this link to access the list:
www.powerkidslinks.com/uptr/bush/